This much anticipated debut collect
demonstrates a remarkable ability to cr

*I Did It Too* collects poems written over
politics of state and person, the city to

C000016607

Featuring commissions from St Paul's Cathedral, Buckingham Palace and Guardian News and well known poems such as *Cog* and *Being British* and the startlingly abrupt *Nowadays*.

*I Did It Too* is a public admittance, a powerful statement at a dramatic moment of history.

Deanna is an international writer, performer and facilitator. She co-curates two leading spoken word events: Chill Pill and Come Rhyme With Me and is on the board of Safe Ground.

Commissions include: Under The Skin (St Paul's Cathedral), Now We Are Here (Young Vic), Women Who Spit (BBC IPlayer) and Buckingham Palace (NYT).

Accolades include: ELLE UK's '30 inspirational women under 30', The Female Lead's '20intheir20s', Cosmopolitan's 'No.1 trailblazing woman', youngest UK Poetry Slam Champion (Farrago 2007/8)

Previous international performances and workshops include: San Miguel Poetry festival (Mexico), Canada (British Council/ Shakespeare lives), Beirut (Roundhouse), South Africa (Connect ZA and Roundhouse), Zimbabwe and Sudan (both British Council).

She teaches the Writing Poetry for Performance module with Benjamin Zephaniah at Brunel University and is a tutor at School of Communication Arts ('The most successful ad school in the world').

Check out her creative experiment Matter: www.thisismatter.com

Instagram/twitter: @deannarodger

Facebook: /deannarodgerpage

# I Did It Too

Deanna Rodger

Burning Eye

BurningEyeBooks
Never Knowingly
Mainstream

This edition published by Burning Eye Books 2017

www.burningeye.co.uk

@burningeyebooks

Burning Eye Books
15 West Hill, Portishead, BS20 6LG

ISBN 978-1-911570-23-3

'I have… I want… I need… and *I can't live without…*'
*Dean Atta and Joe Coelho for all those Monday evenings.*

# CONTENTS

FIRST                              11
PREFACE                            13
NOWADAYS                           17
LONDON LANDLORDS                   19
MONOPOLISED NEWS                   21
LOVE AMBITIONS                     22
THIS IS LONDON, PART 2             24
SILVER FOCUS                       26
TERMINALS                          28
TO TALIESIN                        30
RESUSCITATION                      32
SHE TOOK THE TUBE HOME             34
KIZZLE                             35
INTRANSIGENCE OF DEE               36
SPIKES                             38
TRAINS                             40

HOW TO BE A FEMINIST               42
IPHONE                             45
I TELL HER                         47

GROW WILD 48

BEING BRITISH 50

GRIEF 52

PATERNAL PRAYER 53

CHANGE, YOU SAY 55

COG 56

THIS 59

RECONSTRUCTION 63

MISS RUBY WILD 67

SWIFT KEY 70

INFIDELITY 71

BACCHAE 73

BECKER 74

FADE 76

THIS TEXT: EQUALITY VS EQUITY 77

1432 79

POETRY AS PROTEST 81

MATTER (EXCERPT) 83

# FIRST

My face is pulsing.
By the looks I've been getting it must look repulsing.
That bitch scratched me up good.
I would go back and get her if I could
but it happened last night,
that fateful night
where people got merked and I got hurt.

Visions of being underneath that truck
while kicks were getting aimed and all I could do was duck.
It weren't even my fault, you know, she just switched on me
like a psycho,

pushing me backwards, making me stumble
till eventually I fell down in a tumble and that's when it started,
my head hit the concrete,
her foot hit my head,
fuck this shit, I ain't ending up dead,
so I got up with my cranium so sore and booted that bitch to
the floor
and there she was
in the same position I was moments before.

And there she was in the same position where I was moments
before.

# PREFACE

*I Did It Too*: a collection spanning ten years, from the murky depths of my teenage secret existence to international stages and (open) books.

The title to hold this work together came to me once I remembered that I began writing to admit things.

Most people – well, those I know who have asked (which is most people I know) – will have been led to believe that *Infidelity* was my first poem. It was a more socially acceptable conversation to have:

**Me**: *(straight face, direct eye contact)* My boyfriend told me he had cheated on me and that the girl was pregnant.
**Them:** *(shock face)*
**Me:** Yeah, I was seventeen.
**Them:** *(oh nooo face)*
**Me:** Well *(deep breath in, think 'determined wisdom')*, I saw two choices *(cheeky eye glint)*: destroy, or create.

*I Did It Too* is a collection of admittance.

*First* is actually the first. I wrote it in silent protest to my pissed-off mum. I had been violent; naturally she disapproved. Although I never showed her this rhyme, it made me feel better to get some sort of truth out of my head. A few months later, I was writing all the time.

All the words on the following pages were put in place between the years 2007 and 2017. These are poems which I have performed into mics and ears all over the world. I have been their vessel, able to defend choices and experiences with tonality, gestures and conversation.

And as I type this preface, so close to their printing and binding and uncertain of title and grammar and spelling oversights, I admit I am wondering about you reading these in your brain. What are you thinking of them/me? Will you nod and make that 'mmm' sound? What will you flick to first? What if you don't get me, if you don't hear what I am trying to say?

These poems were written to be said with courage, aloud, to myself then, then to you, and now by you.

'There is a light at the end of the tunnel… hopefully it's not a freight train!'

*Attributed to Mariah Carey*

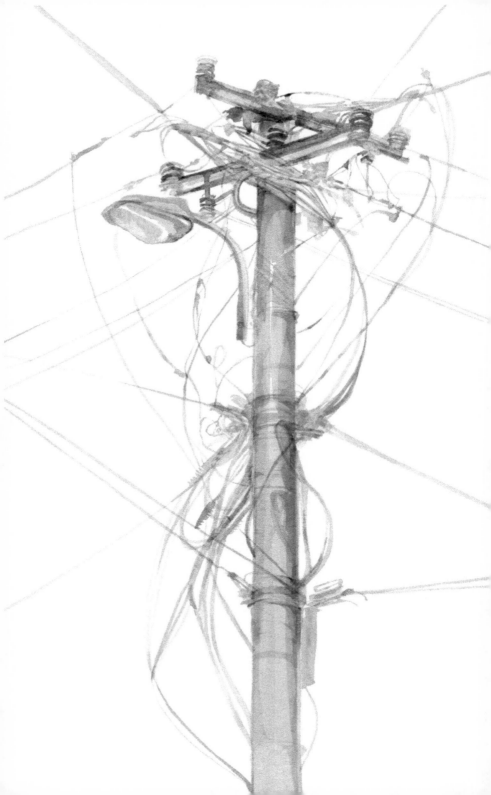

# NOWADAYS

Who cares about voting nowadays?
Nowadays people engage in votes for *Big Brother* and *X Factor,*
masses make records and break them in viewings,
so who cares about elections nowadays?
Nowadays voters wait and watch locked outside as elections count
without them,
so who cares about politicians nowadays?
Nowadays they just perch in their taxpayer-paid-for whatever they
conned out the system
and bitch and moan about benefits who lead the country into deficit
by taking and not giving back,
so who cares about promises nowadays?
'Cause nowadays manifestos are written in jargon by people
detached from the mass,
swallowed in parliament and removed from common language so big
words confuse and diffuse,
'cause no one's got time to read headnote to foot and take notes to
contrast and compare,
no one stares until they see between the lines the lies that hide inside
smiles that style campaigns,
so who cares about truth nowadays?
Nowadays people brave early mornings on body-heated trains to
save possessions they don't really own.
Credit cards are deceiving and bleeding,
victims believing they're needing to live to repay,
so each breath
feeds debt
and their souls become slaves to the pound,
so who cares about protest nowadays?
Nowadays tents are removed from the root and destroyed like weeds
'cause the silence is soiled if the stem breaks free and dreams left to
bloom for ideas to pollinate,
so who cares about nurturing nowadays?
Nowadays the young are babysat by TV screens
and screams are communication 'cause no one listens nowadays,
iPods deafen and stress threatens isolation with problems from
people who don't quite understand
'cause nowadays we are all different
and unique and special and different
but difference is a fear for survival so nobody shares nowadays,
nobody trusts nowadays,
nowadays people travel in bubbles: phone, iPod, free news, or cars.
No eye contact, brief smile, small shuffles and silence.
Who cares about stories nowadays?

Stories that reveal human nature at its peak and expose where we're weak but courageous,
stories of the past before the world spun fast and left day to artificial light.
See, no one really cares about life nowadays.
'Cause nowadays life is a competition where youth is a trophy that should be protected from age.
Where egos are large and injury expected 'cause no one really cares about fun nowadays,
the type of fun you remember and relive in emotion,
not drunken pictures plastered on Facebook,
an optimistic account of a night mentioned proudly on Monday to coworkers who also survive
by drinking then sleeping through weekends so the week never ends and change,
change!
Change is never missed.

So, who cares about voting nowadays?
Those who hope.
Those whose energy is spent trying to defeat odds that are built around them in capitalism and greed.
Those who read and learn and educate minds outside of a structure designed to dictate destinies with narrow paths in concrete labyrinths.

Freedom.
Freedom is often mistaken for the sight of light at the end of a tunnel.
It's the sense that we are free that keeps us trapped.
But who cares about that?

# LONDON LANDLORDS

I am filtering expectations from trying to find my mum.
Cat flap for my cat.
My garden.
Kitchen table.
Downstairs shower, upstairs bathroom.
Desk space.
Play space.
Skylight.

I'm filtering standards.
Keeping a baseline.
Damp visibility free.
Bug free.
Hygienic.
Clean.
Pipe leading outside and underground.
Standard.

Baby boom landlord.
What does the average twenty-four-year-old earn nowadays?
Early mornings, nights late.
London living wage.
How many hours for how many days to earn enough to rent and
save?

I'm filtering locations
to the fringes.
Checking crime rates,
mapping cheap rent.
I'm bearing in mind Oyster card price hikes, the promise of
twenty-four-hour tube and
Night Bus bus routes.

I'm filtering my tax, my phone bill, my travel, my wine,
my hair, my nails, my wax, my charity shop spending,
my Sainsbury habit, my Pret habit,
legal music, Netflix, filter coffee, Kettle Chips.
Capped max, no min searching.

Thatcher's council advantage landlord.
Foreign money buy-to-leave landlord.
Filter your assets.

Hoarders, quicker spenders, many-housed people.
Renter-loaners, ministers.

Sellers of experience.
Inheritors, entrepreneurs.
Grey-suit homers.
Nine-to-five finders, misers that keep pushing and seeing
how much of the market can be squeezed.

Find me a private landlord.
One that invests.
One that shows face,
that'll knock and pop by for a cup of tea to make sure everything
is good
and lovely
and honest.

Find me an honest landlord,
not a stuff-pockets-full-for-the-sake-of-a-footballer's-wage.
Reasonable landlord who'll trust tenants to pay,
not threaten to take the roof away
on those rainy days
when freelance fees are delayed.

Sweet landlord,
please eradicate the estate fees,
decommission the agent,
lower the price per week.

Domesticate us, guardian landlords,
filter our disappointment, filter our restrictions, filter our fitted caps
and raise our standards.
Raise our ambition, our hope, our futures.

Please, loving landlords, imagine us to be your cats,
free to leave and breathe without parents.
Help us start our many lives, London landlords,
knowing the bowl will be filled when we return 'cause we can
afford to fill the fridge.

# MONOPOLISED NEWS

On evenings when the rain is not far away
      and work is tomorrow too soon
there is a space
      for people like me and people like you.

Speakers of this life,
who know the power of sound
      voices in ideas
      word changes
      stand-up manifestos
pen-marked graffiti;    art
wrecking systems of entitlement;    those modern-day arks.

And here you shall meet people like you and like me,
whose days are full of decisions made and worn like summer clothes
   in the rain,

and here you can hear fabrications, tall tales for blooming
laughs
and chatter of love as a wooden splintered chair
and here you can share with people like you and like me

Stories of ships' cargo and white van guests,
      of sunset spotlights, the stages and the dark,
      of how you would save this world, the earth,
      of your jagged thoughts like drowned rocks,
      of grey pigeons across oceans
and ants on top of mountains
and Coke-can wide cities
and politics like clouds, fluff-filled interpreted shapes
and here you can shh the noise of monopolised news
and here we will listen
      to your say,
         your words,
            your sounds,
                your view.

# LOVE AMBITIONS

I wanna be your mirror
so I see what you see, you see what I see and all I see is you gazing at
me.

I wanna be a debilitating disease,
make you weak in the knees, but bless you when you sneeze, and
miss you like a ghost misses form when you leave.

I wanna be the *Big Issue*
man that you give £2.50 to, compassion's material form once held by
you, smell like you, be the scent that you apply, provide the glisten of
desire that resides in your eye,

I want to be your bed,
your sheet, your pillow and cover,
the one that I smother, your bedtime lover, comfort in the form of a
significant other.

Your cocoa butter; invade your pores with the cream of me, just so I
can touch you ubiquitously.
Your pupils; teach me to see that I'm the one for you and you
complete me.

The only Facebook message you'll reply to.
I wanna be the receptor your ligand will bind to.
The pen lids you chew.
Your most comfortable shoes.
The one thing you'll never lose.
The only choice you'll ever choose.
I want to be every single
girl you've ever encountered so that technically,
I'm the only one.

The game you play for fun,
I'll let you monopolise and think that you've won fairly.

Because I wanna be the hand that you lay,
I'll let you handwrite my game. For I wanna be poetry you
write,
a sublimation with a flow that's so tight. Like your boy,
share all instances of carefree joy.
Fight your fights, share your pain, then make it my own.

Your phone; use me to communicate
all feelings of love, loss, despair and hate
For I wanna be soca that makes you whine,
the architect of your love line, please, let me design.

The memory you trigger when you're down.
The riddle you ponder that makes you frown
with confusion, trying to figure the answer.
I'll be your lecturer,
guide to conclusion that it's all 'cause you love her. Me.
Your student ID; I wanna be part of your identity, provide
knowledge, see you need me to get into the library

                                        FUCK IT!


I'd even be your glass            I can only be the woman I am
half-full of Coke and JD,         The woman you see.
if that's all you need from me.

2008                              2013

# THIS IS LONDON, PART 2

London, I see your point.
Your shard steel sky,
your firework smiles,
your laser lights.
Your pace flips my stomach; I yearn to hold you down.
You make me feel like your mistress,
stretched under you, around you, through you.
I know your backdrops and fast routes;
I overstand your underground;
temperamental on Sunday nights,
florescent hall full, music loud, we dance.
In our intimate space, with our foreheads close
and our closed eyes shut, we dance,
you take my hands      and you spin me,
round your core, faster, and faster, ever changing, ever returning
under our time-scarred moon,
our mouths howling like wolves
in your wild wound where
hope hangs in narrow mews hidden between tower blocks;
not warm enough to nestle,
too hard to spring from,
flawless from far.
But London, you are a frantic, relentless, needless addiction
who should know that though I need you I know that you need me
too.
Without me, who will sing you lullabies on late lonely nights,
who will breathe and keep pace with you?
Without me, London,
there would be nobody to see you and agree with your point of view,
no soul to love your incessant core enough to forgive you
for your indeterminable flaws.

My poems taste of you
so I don't hold them in my mouth
my poems read like you
so now I don't hold them in my eyes
my poems write you
so let go

# SILVER FOCUS

I can't remove his face from archives buried in the dark dust of
battles only important to locals.

He is triggered by mixed-race men who wear their sleepless nights
on broad shoulders.

Their eyes are always the prettiest,
their irises kiss skies to life when they wake, and when they die
their eyes are the last to close.
They have the hands of drivers,
the type used to gripping and letting go.
(They are not strong hands.)
They are hands which forget to greet each other,
they don't know how to hold without power,
how to hold without blood.

His hands held me
and I felt the space our bodies battled to hold –
the repellent nature of war,
the wounded lost in the space.
Those hands never felt safe,
their porous nature riddled with dormant pits of fire.
He never lost his temper.
He never had to.
The guns do the frontline firing.

He is archived in the battlefield poppies don't grow in,
where white flags aren't clean enough to raise,
where tortured moments are captured in the prettiest of eyes
like distance doesn't exist.
Like life remembers space,
like I remember him.

I'm frustrated by my hands
only two, and my legs not working properly
how the hips hurt with steps up step up steps
my knees crack from kneeling
my shoulders and back knotted and solid
my neck
shrunken

# TERMINALS

Tonight we will visit a dead man.
We will pretend he is alive.
We will smile.
We will try not to show pity.
We will talk of our pasts.
When asked about our present we will leave out the best parts.
Our futures will not be spoken of.
They do not exist here.
We will be alert to any hint that we should leave.
We will pretend we don't want to.
We won't want to.
We will wish to stay.
To see the peace cover his
face finally.
This is not our right.
We will leave.
I will avoid the eyes of his wife.
She is too alive.
She knows this and
I don't think she will want to be
reminded of her life.
She will be tired.
She will be exhausted by smiling.
Her barriers will remain high.
She will feel damned while we
are sat by her...
He is not dead yet.
I do not know what to call him.
He is at the terminal.
I hope it will be delayed,
but delays are stressful.
I hope it is a smooth sprint along
the runway.
I hope his legs stretch to the
distance of his kindness.

I will forever remember his
height and size.
His gentle nature
and strong hands.
How he allowed us to float in
our dreams as children
and how he built what
cleansed and hid my tears.
I hope he remembers this
also.

He probably doesn't.

I may hum the puff daddy
song he'd sing on repeat.
I miss him more than my dad.
I miss my dad because of
men like him.
I'm missing a man I haven't
seen for years. This is not
unusual.

Men in my life are usually
terminal.
About to leave.

Whether they want to or not.
Whether they should or not
is not the point.

I am used to waving.
Tonight I will wave
with both arms.

# TO TALIESIN

*A thing of beauty is a joy for ever:*
*Its loveliness increases; it will never*
*Pass into nothingness*

John Keats, *Endymion*

His eyes contain a universe. His pupils,
black holes,
pull into the freedom of no thing.
Beauty belongs in the simple being of him.

His beauty could never pass into nothingness,
because his beauty is in the blessing of harvest

and the curse of drought,

the muscle of proud mountains
and the reflective depth in buried lakes,

the shallow tips of waterfalls and icebergs.
The sea, the surge of waves, the thrashing of fish,
the storms of sand and snow,
the scents of breath from flowers' lips.

His beauty is tucked into the circumference of earth,
the rough fringe and chiselled edge,
the battered corners,
the stitched seamline where blue meets green.

He sees the seasons' elements and holds arms up, palms wide to
greet them:
a passionate embrace with summer,
a hasty shake with winter,
a blooming smile for spring and a court for the fall of autumn.

His beauty is in the hush of the old trees that keep stories rooted in
the freedom of the sky.
Coarse trunks stabled by time,
swayed to the excitement of new leaves that leap courageously and
float in current winds.
His beauty is in his music, his movement, his hand married to a
lion's face and experience wrapped round his pulse, his dance,

his art, his disregard for perfection, within perfection,

his liberty to begin again,

the chaotic cohesion of shapes and patterns, the recycled existence of inspiration, him.

Sturdy.

Left behind tooth, dry shaven sideburns, curls that turn to fire in showers and lashes that lie like lazy wishes, timeless smiles, forgiveness, spirit, the deeds that define it. Peace.

His beauty is the defencelessness of sleep.

It lulls my stare of disbelief and lifts my gravity from its intention to distribute it across him, across his plains, his lands, his mountains and oceans and like eagles and sharks, sights are high, for his eyes are the blue cloaks of this earth's universe and each pupil harbours an insatiable depth that takes light from everything and replenishes it as each blink gives birth to a star.

Each tear wipes clear the dark fear of no thing for beauty

simply belongs in the being of him.

# RESUSCITATION

Some homes have to have heart replacements.

They are pink-walled caverns
whose blood locks itself away.
Family-sized blockage.
Failure is a fast-food father.

These holey homes reinforce quarters,
recompose patterns that don't fill like they did before,
pumping loaded cells.
Three kids, one mum.
Two cats.

Stroke.

Memories are gasping breaths, snatching moments.
Limbs bound by pressure machine
squeezing my everything.
Counting home to normal.

Relax, rest.
Room upstairs.
Double,
red,
now
shared,
then
bed single,
skylight.
Floral bedsheets, walls blue.
Bunk bed.
Cat blanket.
Nurse shift.

Food cooked by Tiphanie
fattens the bottom left room,
sister sharing servings.
Spoon, fork, cheese, sauce,
spaghetti whiskers
prechopped.
Who are you after the severance?
Keep heart raised above head to help the blood clot.
When will the phantom syndrome stop?
The numbness ever begin?

The clock locks the door at these hours.
No visitors will arrive, nobody can leave
but the cats.
They breathe a different air.
Their concerns are kept outside the flap which knocks their entrance.

Resuscitation.

They are gas and air and relief.
Their purr is a life support,
our soft spots insulated by their fur.
Like foreign nurses, kindness is a sound,
a rhythm
keeping the pace this home now makes.

# SHE TOOK THE TUBE HOME

She stands inside the doorway of the front room,
the room I am sat in with my plate on my lap,
listening to the programme, watching my phone.

She doesn't say hello.
She doesn't take off her coat.
I shift to show I am willing to move if she wishes to sit.

She chooses to stand.
Suddenly she speaks. She is saying something.
'Sorry, what did you say?'
'Could you turn down your noise?'
'Yes, OK.'
'It's the tube.' She is still talking to me.
'It's literally a human centipede.
People are stuck in something they don't want to be stuck in,
their faces stuck up the arse of someone else, eating and smelling
their shit.
At rush hour, anyhow.' She stops.

'Would you like to sit?' I ask.
'No, I'm fine, thank you.'
'I'm getting up anyway. I insist.'

Her weight shifts from side to side,
left to right to rest and ease her spine:
the polluted river that keeps her up at night.
The source of pain always leads to her mouth.

'The print is as busy as the people,' she adds,
'the people as busy as the print.'
I stand.
From the Macmillan lanyard hanging from her neck, I see her job
involves talking all day to strangers about the excess in their lives.
From her laden eyes I guess today's been mainly about death and the
best way to prevent it.
She sits.

I watch her dig up her sunset in preparation to exhale her day
as right now she sits buried under a mass of needs.
Her eye turns to the time.
I turn to the door
as she sits, as supreme as concrete,
her paths marked by plague, fire and war,
her age apparent in the artificial light,
her cold hands clasp tight, rubbishing her tiny-print maps,
her eyes sleepless,
counting stops.

# KIZZLE

What gives these kids the mentality?
To step out of all reality
and approach this boy so casually,
tear at him so callously,
leave him dying in the street
because they hear the sound of bobs on the beat
on their dicks like dogs on heat,
sirens so slow like this boy's heartbeat,
beat like chimes and pulse is weak.
Tried to run but he couldn't flee.
All he wanted to do was make his p,
work hard and strive for legitimacy,
no daily rate, he wants a salary
because life extorts, it's not pain-free.
Youths fantasise, want what they see on TV
on the crooked, not on the straight street,
living it up with ACB,
coke, weed and ecstasy
like retail thrive in consumity,
doing it bait and conspicuously
so all the kids on the block can see.
Employing their youngers,
crews franchising,
don't take into account the amount of mums crying
plus the older generation that look down sighing
because the youth have gone mad.
Dreams aren't the same.
Ours was freedom.
Why does theirs have to be the hype game?

# INTRANSIGENCE OF DEE

impatient        aggressive        hostile        switchy        bitchy
and        unnecessarily        abrupt        at times
        dark side surfaces        pierces the thing cling
        that feebly attempts to suffocate
        the side of Dee that's a magnet for
        hate


reluctant to participate
rarely tries to cooperate        a tornado        no consideration
        rapscallion


no emotion. no. too much emotion
she sees a watercolour canvas of reds blacks greys
        death's deep stains
lie dormant till scrubbed
        rubbed
external forces release what initially appear as sources
        but the irritation only causes
momentum to build life-binding contracts to be drawn and sealed
warranting her
to flipswitch        act like a bitch, muscles involuntary twitch
        she knows that it's stupid but loves every moment of it
her friends        warn her of the potential risk which
        may arise with the release of this little miss
her reply        'don't take the piss,        can't you see I can handle this?'
her shit
        as she plunges her        fist into a factual brick
        shatters the        mirror to deface
        the image of an actual prick
        habitual dick always fucking up quick
        hit once she switch beat with a sudden twitch
inanimate objects that can't feel won't feel 'cause they don't feel shit
a people parallel,        selfish egocentric mass        of red brick
however you wanna put it        same traits different form


        Dee she
        rejects the norm
        causes a storm
        they the silence
cunning magicianry conjures populations of naive participants into a
        passive compliance
        inhibitors of defiance
        we are hypnotised by tyrants
        into a trance of perfunctory

to do the same shit daily and the same shifts weekly
not seeing our donation to the honey pot of the bourgeoisie
so we do the same shit and the same shifts weekly
all while watching poverty disintegrate into penury
disguised to smell nice
saturated in the scent of quixotic ideology
diffused through tidal waves

flowing through our TVs
mind's sponges absorbing
so-called facts from the BBC

actions dictated
thoughts manipulated

perfect comparison to the Nintendo Wii

puppets in a panic
we wear invisible strings

with precious plastic
our prized possession

we the heat
mould into our creation
what we think
will ease the journey
to our destination

fine clothes fast cars
props of procrastination
dim the creativity of all those in our nation

Dee she
exercises emotions
in a poetic sublimation
a papered production
of her
structured rationalisation
from a blank slate
creates her
customised creation
thoughts                    words
pens                    mic
brain beatboxes a rhythm
a flow of frustration explanation of why I'm
impatient aggressive hostile switchy bitchy and unnecessarily
abrupt.
at times

# SPIKES

The spikes are out.
Tonight a homeless cone
clangs *no change*
into this UK city.

I march past a public perch
built solid concrete slanted,
purpose? Semi-permanent.
*Sit here for a second*, it says.
*Slide here, don't stay.*

Walk past
box office doors
that extort bums
to watch make-believe.

Setting method spikes
beneath backstage shelter
to stop rough sleeping from dreaming for stall seats
after the applause is done,
after the make-up's wiped clean,
after the staff have locked up the cash thresholds
that entertain the silver studs of the six rich borough codes.

The rain has lost its way,
landing on my lap as I'm sat on the bus stop bench
by closed tubes,
it's late
and I am confused by this bus stop roof
angled open wide.
I'm staring up like
maybe the rain don't fall right,
maybe it's built wrong,
maybe it's the wind cuts chucking nature's funding buckets over this
defensive design,
transient shelter justice,
Tory benefit
for those draughty drifters that roam the road for rights,
begging pedestrians,
scavenging scapegoats
find free news to think of
between the run home
from work to work, from home to shop,
home from friends to pub

from debt from bills to home from
heads stress-full with stuff,
no time to read the signs from ads
marketing humanity with cold calcified hands.

We don't hear the cone clang clang change clang clang
hey look at me on this cardboard carpet clang make-believe home on
this floor that spike-heeled souls chip,
see me
in the corner of the road and the wall,
see here the corporate drains full, the heavy red light,
hear the high-pitched breath of businesses that suggest our cities to
be owned by the half-percent that spend on this...
architecture that's selfish, hostile,
exists to disrupt, not support with peace,
policed out of sight, forced to leave.
Antisocial law deems right to rest illegal –
sheltered pavements attract nuisance,
window ledges are for flogging,
home has no room in the privatised public space,
locked out living on floor spikes.

No home is no choice for the tenant.
An intentional sofa subsidence,
traffic exhaust is central heating,
British weather water bills,
food bank fridges,
rucksack wardrobes,
bag beds,
hat accounts, kicked in,
kicked out, kicked off, move on.
Asbo.
Don't be seen living here make-believing home clang change
clang go, slip away out of sight outside of this UK 2k15 city night.

# TRAINS

Things to remember when you are on the platform staring at the tracks:
one giant step for you is a leap for their hearts and you will be missed far more than you will miss this,
and this should keep you here to get to know yourself how they know you.

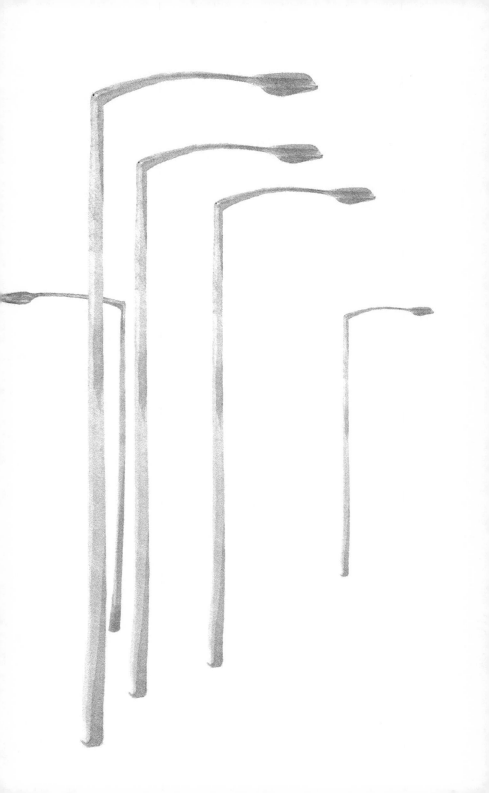

# HOW TO BE A FEMINIST

Want what I haven't got.

Wear what I want.
Short skirts.
Low tops.
High heels.
(Fuck the twat that said not to wear high heels so the creepy
shadow man can't hear me, they are a weapon and if my knees
and hips weren't so bad I would wear them more often because
high heels are boom and it's mainly because of the walk and
click they make.)

Love women
who own their bodies and their rights and their homes and their
cars and their bus pass.

Let armpit hair grow free.
Shave and wax and epilate when the friction becomes an irritant.

Paint nails.
Don't hide the chip.

Wear deodorant but don't look like I do.
Be invisible.

Don't be invisible.
Hate women
when they decide they don't agree with me.

Hate myself.

When nobody notices me,
love my sexy body.
Have sex.
Don't apologise.
Be 'free'.

Sleep with boyfriends, male friends, friends of friends, cheaters
and foreigners, liars and dealers, drummers and rappers, players
and professionals.
Don't feel like a whore.
Get drunk and fuck everyone
at the same time
in a tent.
Wake up and

42

leave them – before breakfast if possible.
If not,

don't wash the dishes.
Never wash the dishes
until there are no more dishes.
Love men

who carry bags
and pay for things
and go down
and cook
and listen
and agree.
Hate dicks

when they decide they don't want to be with us
and their mouths turn into giant arseholes that want to suck our
matter in to fart their gas out.

Fart, belch, don't giggle, stern face,
subtweet and avoid confrontation, bitch.
Don't use the word *bitch* unless chanting a hip-hop song.
Don't let anyone use the word *bitch* unless quoting a male
rapper.
Call Beyoncé and Rihanna my bitches 'cause they obviously
don't mind.
Become a role model.
Be a feminist.

Never stop changing.
Don't forget.
Let go.
Forgive.
Expect whistles and slow cars,
accept but don't slow for them.
Boast in conversations
over every sound.
Think before you speak.
Create judgement.
Answer.
Retweet.
Form an army of followers.
Unfollow unfollowers.
Lead.
Be strong.

Be happy.
Be thin.
Run.
Date,
and be grateful.
Don't piss on the seat.
Don't sit on the seat.
Wipe the piss off the seat.
Hate 'Shewees' – stand for squatting.
Demand safe night toilets for women.
Don't be embarrassed by your tampon.
Pay for your period.
Buy stress.
Follow trends.
Try 'Shewees' – hate street lights.
Laugh loudly and shout, fall over other women.
Scrabble to stand tall.
Be opinionated.
Form an opinion.
Buy it with the second round of rosé and sambuca shots.
Be intelligent, witty, pretty, sharp, judgemental, blunt.
Possess an opinion.
Get noticed through it.
Throw it up like regurgitated 3am chips on a bus, falling out of a
sexy dress and high heels.
@everyone
#Gethomesafe.
It's your right, to get home safe.
Write it
but don't read the comments.

Never read the comments.

# IPHONE

Her boyfriend hung up the phone on her.
Said he couldn't hear her,
though he sounded clear to her ear.
He stuttered his excuse.
'I can't hear you.
You're breaking up.
Stand somewhere, anywhere other than where you have chosen to.'
She obediently lined up,
aiming his name
like a one-girl game of money up.
Her lucky penny.
Flicked high, somersaulting through space, confidently falling head
over heels,
but it didn't land right.
It bounced back,
tails up.
He hung up.
She lay down face up,
resigned to redial as ring-rings, ring-rings, ring-rings ran round
chasing his voicemail,
pleading him to shout into her vessel and make echoes bounce
around like change.
Hollow, she begged his investment to fall in
and splash her sides with stories she could use,
to numb her captive thumbs and soothe silence through his sounds.
She craved his dependence like the sweet nothings
she'd taste on her tongue in the addictive way that as lovers they'd
kiss passionately
in the emptiness of dark streets on long nights that daylight put to
sleep.

When he called back,
closed eyes,
scratched touch screen with gloved finger, aware identity,
her identity's prints were to be taken,
to be cloned, to be spread.
But resistance can't exist without vulnerability,
so, fingertip stripped,
it tipped the marker to the right and she picked up.
He was too weak to greet her,
too fatigued to say her name,
blocked up and
in need of a prescription she hadn't heard of.
Their conversation worsened.
She felt it in the way her arm trembled from the phone held in hand

held to head.
Dead weight.
She was breathing, forcing life into a corpse.
But as she sighed her last 'I love you'
she saw his whisper:
'Just trust me.'
Assured, she stored those words,
insured them for four, to ensure alarm would guard.
Her alarm flashed light, on silent, nine times,
when thirty-six prods from his inquisitive prints obscured the perfect
black of their infinity
but, regardless of how her eyes would sting in brightness, they'd
adjust in fast blinks, scattering tones until they found before beneath
and she'd reread, reread, reread
'Just trust me.'
She'd reread, reread, reread
'Just trust me'
as access denied his eleven symbols her sight.
Because his credit ran dry.
She rereads, rereads, rereads
'Just trust me'
as she realises she has signed into
a sacred IOU,
idolised his pay-as-you-go as a contract.
She rereads, rereads
his small print written in metaphor,
rereads,
his signature a duplicate picture of a kiss,
'Just trust'
the line cut out
after the signal crackled with the last spit
'me.'
She called.
She calls.
She's calling for him to answer.
'I can't.
I can't hear you.
We're breaking up.'

# I TELL HER

I tell her
if she does her homework she can be whatever she chooses to be.
She doesn't believe me, says she'll stay stupid for the rest of her life
while watching the *Wizards of Waverly Place* on a 42" paper-thin HD
TV
My voice gets hung as my heart falls off the cliff of her broken esteem.
'Of course you're not stupid.'
'Everyone thinks I am.'
'Well, I'm everyone and I don't, so you're not.'
'My mum does.'
That there is a full stop.
I try to pull it down into a comma.
'I'm sure she didn't mean…'
But like an overpulled spring she recoils and buries her head back
into her tent of opened umbrellas and heart-covered blankets.

There is no use in telling her that an umbrella opened indoors is bad
luck.
She already knows.
She just wishes for any luck,
and the umbrella serves the same purpose as if she was stood in
torrential rain.
She can't help feeling damp, but she can block the attack.
I follow her,
half in, half out, 50:50.
It's the best I can do due to divided loyalties, a grown-up perspective.
I'm an alien invading her way of living.
She has everything, wants for nothing,
tantrums and screams and slams and threats cave her parents in
and so her room is full of plastic phases and half-opened cases
displaced but replacing
*nos, stops, enoughs.*

I'm still facing the most privileged little girl I have ever met.
But she already knows the price of inanimation, so I tell her she is
loved,
she is funny and kind and beautiful,
she is intelligent and if there is one lesson she simply must revise for,
it's life.
She smiles.
'Dee,' she says,
'you always say things that don't make sense but make me smile.'
I smile back and say,
'Life doesn't make sense straight away,
but if you remember the things that make you smile then you can
smile always.'

## GROW WILD

And free and fill the cracks with

med-**i**-cinal

# roots

Sprout **green** and *yellow* and **purple** and w h i t e

And bright                    *feral* and lum!nous

glow in the **dark times** of life on this planet

       The soil is

# nuclear

                    cement is
                    air-caged

Grow up       grow   brave

Grow **billowing** *proud*

Grow whisper bonkers
    crooked and matted and perfect and leave
       the earth with your fuzzy spawn untamed unkempt
relax
Spring into wind tingling chlorophyll!!!!
Rocket
   launch
     the rain baths
     sodden soil!!!

Breathe        through        your                    pores.

*Grow how you feel,* SUNSHINE.

Grow LIFE

Grow   **W.....I.....L.....D.**

# BEING BRITISH

I always get asked,
'Where do you come from?'
My repeated reply is
'London.

The town that sheltered a mother fleeing from war-torn land,
baby in belly given chance to be a man,
a city of prosperity.
She sought jobs allowing her to keep her dignity, independently
living in a state,
*not off it.*
Her benefit,
one son,
a bright boy of renewable energy.
He knew all he'd ever be
was a product of the city that changed his destiny.'

'OK,'
they say,
'but what country?'
I breathe deeply,

swallowing sarcastic syllables, and exhale,
'Great Britain.
The island
throned in seas that        channelled safety.
She carried men to defend
countrysides scattered with towns full of factories.
The curator of colonies
voiced view to keep view,
exploit used to heavily recruit
natural warlikes
to fight aggressively,
with strength and bravery.
Fifty-two thousand casualties,
Ghurkhas' support
over two world wars.
Nearly half a million fought for
Great Britain.'

I'm teasing them,
because although it's not a lie
I know it's not the desired response
and so am not surprised when they reply,
'Where are your parents from?'

See, I can't hide pigment skin within words,
whether fact or fiction.
So I tell them
I'm a product of miscegenation.
That my parents' parents are from Jamaica and Scotland.
Raised in England,
they found love and made life in London
to birth and breed a British girl.

So while I'm an addict for hard food,
I fiend for the smell of 'eggs an' ba'on' in the morning,
I'm a sucker for a cuppa
and I'll batter a fish and chips in less than fifteen minutes.
I was raised by the church and educated by *EastEnders*.
Friday nights of teenage life were spent going on drink benders.
I can't pretend, 'cause
all I know is GB
and I suppose on paper I could quite possibly read as
an ideal recruit in the BNP,
wear my balaclava too high so my eyes can't see
the route of my journey to the RWB,
ticket's the qualifications on my CRB,
five for hate crimes would get me VIP.

But a face-to-face interview
would refuse my application
on the grounds that those I walk on are not my birthright nation,
profile is proof of racial integration,
defies the silent slogan of skin-based segregation
and as the tick box of White/Caribbean is crossed
my rights are wrong and I should politely get lost.

Pack bags,
try to find where I belong.
But before I'm forced to leave
I'll leave thoughts to ponder on.
Where do you, your parents
and your ancestors come from?

# GRIEF

I run away from it to write about it behind its back.
I am selfish when I hear that someone has passed.
I wish their passing to me.
I think about the people I have seen pass before.
I do not think of the grief.
Who cares about what grief they are holding when I have held it
too?
Why must we have an evening of sad talk when I wanted romance
and weed?
Shall I smoke now,
alone, or bring in those who hold back tears and words?
Cry, for Christ's sake, cry,
let it out, talk,
I can't sit by you wanting to ask about the person who is no
longer
here,

                          you must tell us.


                                                    I can't
        sit by you wanting to ask about the person who is no longer here.
                                    Let it out, talk,
                              cry, for Christ's sake, cry
                  alone or bring in those who hold back tears and words.
                                    Shall I smoke now?
                          Why must we have an evening of sad talk
                              when I wanted romance and weed?
                          Who cares about what grief they are holding
                                    when I have held it too?
                              I do not think of the grief.
              I think about the people I have seen pass before.
                              I wish their passing to me.
    I am selfish when I hear that someone has passed. I run away from
                        it to write about it behind its back.

# PATERNAL PRAYER

Forgive me, Father, for I have sinned.
When I was eight
I stole my granny's fags.
I lied, I swore, I cursed during my time at Lady Mags.
Often got prang just in case they searched my bags,
see, I didn't have the money so I would often pop the tags.
I'm sorry that I'm not perfect
and that I sometimes let you down,
but do you know what, Father?
I just need to come around
to the fact that you're not here with me
and though I can't see you I still have to believe
and the issue that I can't hear you.
Even though my little brother seems to.
Father and son united in sport,
me and my sister you seem to have forgotten,
unanswered prayers left lying there,
presents sent back still fully wrapped,
unwanted,
no love,
just like the day you walked out without a goodbye
even though you saw me see you punch my mother in her right eye
and I remember the time that you tried to embarrass me,
jester dressed like a king
performing in front of my family,
dialling my number
ready to diss,
chat shit on the line to try to take the piss,
adamant to hear my voice shake.
I gave it all I could but there was no more I could take.
See, I'm usually stubborn to your preschool games, but this time
tears welled, dams destroyed, flooding me with shame.
In your element 'cause I had finally succumbed,
got me crying on loudspeaker,
golly, that must have been fun,
but it's all good 'cause I pressed on, stayed strong,
waded through the bull, inhaled this shit like I am toking on a bong,
for you see, Father,
I know what I want
and it's not what you've written 'cause that's not in my font.
I write essays while you take notes,
I sail ships while you row boats,
through the correct method of induction I form my theory,
though confounders try to confound I hold them constant so I see
clearly

'cause there's been many a time where I've felt to quit, sit,
light my spliff, take a hit, fuck this shit and get out this bitch,
live the fast life, fuck the strain and strife, get on my hustle
'cause I can't stand the nine-to-five
but I couldn't do that 'cause I said I'd
press on, stay strong, focus on the right and do no wrong,
live life to the full, no regret or no hate, what's in store for the future
I anticipate, have an open mind, hold an open heart, 'cause as I see it
it's ignorance of others which is driving this city apart.
All these deaths have got me to ponder,
put pen to paper and let my mind wander.
What if it was different and we never went to war?
Would youths still reject and have no respect for the law?
Would they still hold knives and guns like they are soldiers,
follow thugs and act up 'cause they wanna be olders,
kill a different colour 'cause they are on another side,
think that it's cool to take MAC-10s for a ride
'cause they see it on TV
live in Iraq, Bush and Blair sent them there so they can do that?
But these are just my thoughts as I lie upon my bed,
offered to you, God, in an attempt to clear my head.
See, there's sirens in the background but relief in my soul
'cause it's not my little brother isolated in that hole,
luck of a widow when he took the dice to roll,
landed on six and the devil took its toll.
Another day, another death, that's what media would say,
a journalistic account designed to bring shame,
unnatural causes, that's what postmortem would say
a simple statement juxtaposed next to my pain.
It's not fucking fair,
that's what I'd exclaim,
and when are we gonna realise that it's time for a change,
to feel the rucksack of anxiety evaporate in your rays,
show appreciation and give thanks for all of our days
and have faith that there are many more to come?

# CHANGE, YOU SAY

'Change,' you say.
Change how?
When poverty has got us sinking deeper into the dark places of life
like
the cheap is luxury when you can hardly afford to feed your kids,
what choice does melancholy leave
when exhaustion prevents sleep?
And what choice do the councils keep from the vulnerable at the
bottom of the heap?
And tell me how to build a home when you are reminded it ain't
your property,
and don't tell me home is in my bones, my eyes, my mind.
Don't tell me that it's mine to find inside
my body,
my blackened body,
overcrowded limbs, flattened mind,
buggy legs,
lay me in vermin in your liquor-numb arms,
decanter me from slums,
squalor-level private sector
hidden behind four days of bleach and everything is fine, everything
is OK,
it's OK, pay what you can barely afford,
stress free market enriched with capped benefit.
So knock on atoms' doors 'cause heaven's gates are unregulated,
bashing, screaming, split apart, let us in
to the future.
Let us in to the past.
Let us in to more time to find rent and find peace of mind.
How did we get locked out of our own lives?
How did we miss the blue letters, the sold-out council letters?
I'm sorry, Miss Single Person, you're not high priority.
I apologise, couple nine-to-five,
your pay package doesn't disguise the arrears you've racked up,
intentional home-losers,
and, family of five, be satisfied
your doors let the world in as you would like us to do for you
and so put up with tarpaulin roofs,
contagious damp and leaking wires,
put up with what you can't afford to lose.

# COG

I never wanted to see the change.

The shift.
The sides.
The divide.
The offence.

I try to remember the moment colours were used as a guide.

Primary school:
PE in leggings – 'Why does your bum stick out?'
Spice Girls – 'You can't be Baby Spice, your hair's not blonde, you have to be Scary.'
Fancying the brown boy was an insult we would throw at each other like lurgies.

I decided I wouldn't choose sides.

Secondary school:
striped blazer,
pink shirt, black skirt,
slicked frizz.

I insisted it would never define me.

Heavy hip-hop beats,
fresh words expressed,
called back, called out, reprimanded,
mocked by posh girls and teachers.

Speak like a lady.

College:
shift,
mixed, boys and culture.
short skirts, make-up, high heels.

Knowing that it's just a show, an attraction, an image.

Tracksuits, trainers, rucksacks.
Mandem spudded to ensure no misunderstandings about how far I wished to go.
Blud, fam, bredrin greetings.
Defence mechanisms, counteracting bikini bold availability.

It's hard out here. It's been hard for years.

And now there's an arse/bum in my face,
champagne displays,
money-stuffed bras,
a bitch/black woman on all fours

And now I'm trolling, offended, filled with rage.

@ing my tweets, blatant calls.
No private.
No point in hiding.
I'll follow you.

Lighthearted objectification.

I'll draw a map of where you got lost in your attempt at satire.
Where you found racism.
Where misogyny chirpsed you and led you to his car.
Where you pimped our gender.

Where my colour became your bitch.

I'm croak-toned to my mum who is telling me
that there are worse things in the world,
that I have enough to think about,
that not everyone thinks the same.

I am only one girl.

And I am screaming at my white mum telling her I am black
and I am a woman, and for the past twenty-four years
I've been facing these racist slurs every day
and I have done my best to ignore it.

To charge through the barriers.

To play safe and silent.
To smile at comments and blacked-up faces.
To question bigotry and label it ignorance.
To cool my burnt rage and take the blame.

To find a filter that fits all.

'That's not sexist, it's banter.
She's not racist, but
big butts are whippable.
A view's a view.

Ask the women, there was no pressure.

It's satire.
Tongue-in-cheek.

A bit of fun.
But I have a brain and cellulite, so I don't shake my bum on screen,

but if I could I would,' you say.

But you chose not to.
Mortgage paid?
Kids set up? No pressure on you to.
So this privileged jest is just too much.

I'm not easily offended but I have had enough.

And I am crying for all those who will never understand.
Who will never feel a weighted colour of skin.
Who are white even if they tan.
Whose perspectives can't protect me 'cause they can't see.

The echoes of those that watch these videos and say,

'I think you need to chill out.
I guess I have to see it before I believe.
Let it go, breathe.
Surely it's a joke.

Meant to be empowering, a statement.

Her heart was in the right place.
She wasn't thinking about race.
She didn't do the casting.
It's not her fault, she has no control.

She's a big cog in a bigger system.'

# THIS

I guess I'm finally able to admit that
what I wanted so badly as a kid was
money and fame and recognition
for being great from everyone.
And now I've seen that this is frivolous and sensed I must shift tack,
sensibly mock the made-up carbon stars, press parties, publicity,
the visible mystery in between,
humans blown up to be
super-cool
timezone commuters
sailing silver screens as protagonists.

The life of my dreams is to be that celebrity. And recently, I've taken
to talking to shamans and psychics,
wanting them to say this,
say that one day
you will save us all.
Know that you are powerful and magical and you've just forgotten,
just need to recall who you are,
just need to trust that luck cannot run out or away or be anything
other than a faith.
Remember that you create this world with your thoughts and
thinking and words and energy.
You are God source energy, that's what was said to me.
And this is grand,
and I'm grateful
as it made me smile,
but tell me more? Please continue.
What should I do with my God source?
How do I use it?
Can I still abuse the smoke and ritual of lost thought wandering
through
reels of despair where there doesn't need to be,
of trigger-happy sirens and refugees,
of fickle fear and floods and drought and offensive denial
from elite fuckers who keep fracking humanity
into right and black, rich and poor, ruler and ruled,
a dual of comparison and desire and lack?

And right now
I reflect a witness to all of this.
Passive ignorant hypocrites
wishing for a kid's perspective,
a bubble-safe, riptide narrative,

drift while they drown,
privileged injustice,
accurate mistake,
couldn't just make it up,
the triumph of love,
them saving us, us moral beasts.
Retell me our myth of peace and our piece of it,
home office,
citizenship,
coast court judgement.
Your crime is forgetting your senses.
Inhuman.
Change in isolation,
return to the cell to remember the tune
taught to you, before you slept in this air,
before form slit your thought
and process split your soul.
Time seeker,
swear an oath to God that you never knew
solar son would suffocate shadow.
'Objection.
Clouded judgement.'
Tell me the truth about you,
about the        moments you've faked.
How many strokes to minutes,
bigoted seconds of compliance,
were you struck by silence?
The weapon of choice, of skill, of experience.

Light jury,
you're responsible for care for detail,
for probably possible, possible not probable,
for knowing the difference
between heat and opinion,
and rain swaying changing minds,
for staying for days of complaining for the divine,
for lucky democracy,
incarceration for liberty.
Free the universe, the air of transparency.
Charge the capitalist education about what we breathe,
where it's from and what we can become,
sentence the pound of politicians' flesh.
Their queen's head.
The image of something worth working for,
the coloniser's narrative.
Don't judge this cognitive pilgrimage to be superfluous and dramatic.

It's the verdict of an attention-seeking kid needing to be more than
she is told she is.
Judge that and bring to light the cause of it.
The relevant abruption of this is how I choose to live documentaries
and award acceptance speeches which admit that deep
in the starved abyss of nostalgic fantasies
we all
wanted this.

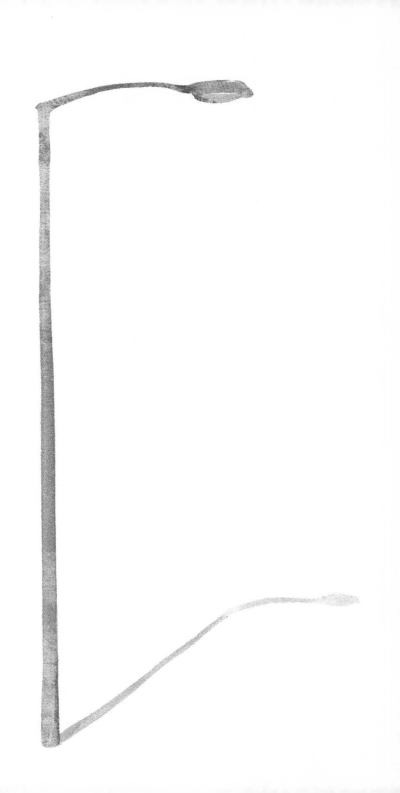

# RECONSTRUCTION

A Mother and Child rest as still as peace by the angels,
their sole flat on a marble circle.
Sculptures make the viewer their subject. They direct:

*Circle us when you visit us,*
*encompass our dimensions,*
*do not speak of one side*
*as our perspective. Tourist,*
*do not miss the point.*
*Do not judge our existence as economical,*
*move around us as Earth is forced to,*
*as you once believed the sun to.*
*Think forward past presumptions, look about you.*
*Reimagine us at every degree.*
*We are your creation:*
*formation of birth and martyrs, prophecy and wars.*
*Hear this and know that these things matter,*
*that we are life source.*

*Phoenix masons,*
*those who have mastered how to house the dead*
*and deliver them the presence of the living.*
*The detail is sacred.*

Christopher Wren,
an astronomer turned architect,
returned from Paris in 1666 to a fire-eaten city
with redevelopment plans in hand.
His precision built this dome from his mind.

Regeneration of the old design.

Who could have predicted it?
What does his astral natal chart read?
Where were the star signs and planets at the time of his birth?
Did he ever configure how the circles and houses aligned into
prophecy?

A pilot for shock and awe tactic – an attempted gentrification?

London,
tell him his dome is not impressive, say it.
He will know you to be lying.
Tell him you don't gasp like a suckling child when you look up,
tell him that you don't crave its life.

Immortalised.

Wren knew how to rewrite,
a surprise saviour,
courage and luck, and divine intervention.
He who marks the star paths and predicts their patterns
finds flow in fire and life in ash.

What survived the 1941 Blitz?
Who saw six men digging out a 4,400-pound bomb
to preserve St Paul's?
Who now lives in the shock,
the 100-foot crater left by the explosion of Hackney Marshes?

Who knew John Donne's statue would be buried in books,
that they would burn protecting him,
that modern-day students would become dumb to reciting their own
narratives?

Is this the point of genesis?

London's city suckled and grew.

Age sediments thought, till forgotten
who they came from,
who they served.
Tracing patterns, this is nature.
Relics become stories, truths
identity finds hard to let go.

How do you breathe beneath the domed layer of weight fumes and
organ sounds?
Can you release your soul from gravity?
How can you not shape presence in the incense of the sky?

Saturn moves into Sagittarius.
Squares Neptune – natural law.

Roof reinforcement.
Rafter reconstruction.
New generation, choose your materials:

- Courage to redesign your city,
- Privilege and drive to draw and lay down plans,
- Magic to conjure design through rejection.

Who's done this?
Who knows themselves as God?
Who believes this to be true?
Who manifests places of worship and sanctuary, heavens and
homes?
Who controls sight, what is foreseen?
Whose reality is anything other than a membrane interpretation?
A constant state of receiving and giving, of sorting, of trusting,
disciples of blind faith and so

are we not schemas of knowing nothing but what we create?

Howard, Collins, Nightingale. Heroes.
The dead are lowered above Florence's head.
(My commission research notes have balance and instinct written
into them.
Heal this. Break chains which hold progression in suspense.
Memorialise these figures in instinct.)

I do not know my history well enough to evidence
my reluctance at praising warlords and their huge tombs.

Wellington, Nelson: curators of heroic acts.

What will you build before you die?
How will you affect the living?

Wandering past memorials of war,
of 'saviour' giants and 'poor small Indians'.
How much is learnt from this through seeing?

*Here is a war which will end all wars.*
*Here we are today still in wars.*
*The satellites now circling.*
*The drones now killing.*
*People now dying.*
*People now fleeing.*

*Before map apps, it was star paths.*
*Before flashlights, it was moonlight.*

Make it

where we want to experience this human world.
Make it
where we want to meet the pain,
the best pulpit for the art of shocking news,
of refugees and of martyrs – witness – perspective.

Mass media turns us into the martyrs of other people's suffering.

Keep the views flooding in.
Keep the contemporary pieces coming in, showcasing
the other's existence.
Guardian mirrors seem to know them well.
Take time to observe all angles,
to fall for every independent degree.

Now,

ask your soul,
the part of you hidden from the rest of the world,
hidden from yourself on most days,
ask that part,
'How well do you remember the love you exploded through?
The tunnel you travelled through to arrive here,
crying trauma on both sides.
Praised in a foreign language.
Patiently fed to peace.
Hums spiralling lullabies from the heavens of some dome.

What do the alive know about living?
How shall we save ourselves before we die?'

# MISS RUBY WILD

**From: deanna rodger <dmkr@hotmail.co.uk>**
**To: missrubywild@me.com**
Date: Friday, August 8, 2014
Subject: happening isn't it

It is winter in South Africa.
I knew this but I didn't think that it would be cold enough to shiver.
The wind cuts like London but clearer.
There are less cars here.
Parking seems to be easy.
You pull up anywhere and a man in a fluorescent pops out.
He protects your car for rands,
as many as you can give him.
I'm not sure that this is an official job.

I was expecting extreme here,
and it is in a way.
When we were driving up to The Joburg it looked like a 1980s
futurist design,
dirty-ice-grey blocks
piled on top close together,
like how do you get in?
Ring roads all around and over each other,
double-decker flyovers.
It's crazy to see. I took a picture. It doesn't quite capture it.
The energy, the chaos, the taxis, craft beer trendiness,
the construction builders recycling,
the art.
Photos never do.
We are staying in the easyHotel.
Pip's got cockroaches,
so I like my room the best.
We've not stopped moving since we got here.
The workshops began yesterday.

Workshop plan.
Intro.
Who am I?
Where did I come from?
Why are we doing this?
What is home?
Where can I find it?
Sorry, who are you?
Let's perform.

Pass the air.
See it become something.
Change it with your hands.
Believe in that change.
Pass that belief on.
Speed-write.
What is home like for you here? Where do you live? And where is that? Gated communities? What are the suburbs? Where are the townships? What is it like to grow there?

**To: missrubywild@me.com**
I took the Virgin Mary you brought me out last night and
my gosh did we boogie in Soweto, those South Africans know how to party!!!
Everything kitted out to the max.
I got my nails painted and a T-shirt made for free,
I didn't get a green Sprite rucksack, the poisonous goodie bag,
it made me think of divide and conquer.
I was jealous and in hope.


Now I'm in Stellenbraam, a university town near to Cape Town.
It is where the apartheid was thought up and
seven of the eight prime ministers during apartheid studied here.
It stinks of it. It's everywhere.
The trees breathe it.
I see it in the workers.
The workers!
I am calling them workers. Here nine hours and it's got my words.
I've time-travelled with a smartphone,
cars rattle the windows,
the toilet water wouldn't stop earlier.
I didn't want to drink the water from the tap;
its structure is Joburg's black night, Stellenbraam's fear.

The trees speak different here.
I am stood under a punishment tree,
saw the stump
chopped at the front.
The palm tree whip lines,
these do not tell age,
these do not lend themselves to writers.
I do not know the names of the slaves, the men, the women
sold by these trees on this patch of green which has no sign,
no remembrance.

**missrubywild@me.com,**
Stellenbraam is not Stellenbraam, it's actually called Stellenbosch.
I called it Strassbosch in the workshop,
the kids laughed and told me what it is.
Also there were seven prime ministers, not eight,
though the ratio is the same.

Where is home on your body?
Where would your bedroom be?
The naughty step on the foot 'cause no one cares about those,
and what about your heart kitchen,
lung garden?
What objects?
What feelings?
Where would you place them? Impatient legs,
magnetic soles.
Wipe your feet at my throat.

This pub has a tree whose branches are a matted roof.
The trees aren't comfortable here, they have cancer.
Sometimes I think this world has cancer,
bad cells not deleting each other.
I'm thinking the cancer is the deformation of the universe,
where antimatter wins.

We spoke of oceans,
how the Indian and the Atlantic meet at Cape Point;
I saw this as a metaphor.
Taz said, 'Our beautiful mountains capture water,
it's the best to drink.
These mountains know how to cry.'

I feel like I am on a fault line.
Like the two oceans swim separately under these mountains.
Like the mountains have been swept up by force and forced to sit
here for tourist photos,
picturing peace, not able to capture it.

**missrubywild@me.com,**
stay focused on the present.
The only boundary is our breath, so keep breathing.
Deep from the roots,
these trees aren't talking right, right here.
We will breathe their growth.
Home tomorrow and I'm thinking,
what if the whole world were to breathe at the same pace?

# SWIFT KEY

There are some words that I dare not say aloud.
The little ones that seem too vulnerable.
The echoes that sound too proud.

They can jump out loud and excitedly
or seep out meek and quietly
to tell the thought trails of feeling. Sometimes they aren't enough,
so to translate exactly what we feel,
sometimes it feels like we say too much.

A warfare of diction
where losing can feel like a loss of larynx
and success is a force-fed megaphone,
words amplified from mouth,
embellished quotes retold pull-out sentences,
and this contradicted chain of sounds,
this lexicon of harmoniously discorded syntax
is native.

And I admire it for the evolution it forces,
rediscovering words as shapes blocked when felt,
typing on light screens, touching fingers to what lies beneath, leaving
imprints,
printing patterns that remember our past and tell present, suggesting
futures.

Sliding with swift keys we open our personal dictionaries of intention
and I message predictably,
*Love you, I really and completely truly do.*

# INFIDELITY

I never thought it would have
made me feel so sad,
so distressed that my best friend and love,
bond strong like a fist in the midst of a titanium glove,
could and then would
sex someone else
with no thought of me, just himself.

*December,*

you answer, is when it happened,
and you don't know, 'it just sort of, well, kind of just happened.'
Well, did I come to mind when she was on the bed flattened
or is this a regular occurrence which has developed and patterned?
*Was I boring?*
Questions ransack my mind,
searching for answers, so desperate to find,
'cause what you just said caused my heart to bind,
wires bound round so tight that it's imposs to unwind,
can't
and won't unwind. I need to stay on guard,
soldiers surround, imposters are barred,
scaffolding holds together pieces broken and scarred
whilst mind forces self to feel happy and to laugh
'cause what's done is done,
we cannot change the past,
nor can I think that this pain will last.
I've got to hold my head high and move on fast,
put on a front and wear a facade
'cause you don't understand how I felt about you,
you can't even begin to comprehend the extent to which I truly loved
you
and despite mind's might to take flight
I still do.
'Cause truth spoke when I said you were my best friend,
I won't take that back,
but I can't fuck with fiction, got to focus on facts.

Fact you fucked her,
there's nothing more to say.
Fact she didn't take the CP the very next day,
nor did she take it the day after that,
so it's a fact that in six months she'll be quite fat.
It's a fact that we can't be together again
and a shame 'cause I've now lost all faith in men

seeing them so weak because pussy makes them purr
and you're just like them 'cause you purred after her

but
it's true when you say I've got something to hide 'cause I too
have a secret rooted deep down inside.
I did do it too,
I did just let go,
I did say yes when I should have said no,
so, though it burns, I understand
and I kind of know why you took her hand,
went with the flow, all actions unplanned,
'cause I've got reasons why I took his
and it wasn't an attempt to hurt or to diss,
not premeditated, just a sudden kiss
stimulated by sex-scented smell of bliss

and as the heat of the moment condensed as a mist
and
I looked into his eyes
I realised I was pissed,
a compulsive component of character I'd missed,
the paramount power, we both should have had, to resist.

# BACCHAE

to be seen and heard
not sit and smile
to scorn and scream and laugh and cry
and work and play
and flirt and run
and preen and dance and drink and smoke
and lie and please
and twirl and grin at bants
and hurt
and hurt you too
and cheat and date and call, text first and
breathe and speak to just be heard

we are Bacchae women
and girls and banshees and mistresses and lovers
and mums and daughters
and cousins
and sisters and heirs
and rich and poor and one with all
does my sexiness upset you
can I shit and burp
and mock the red-blushed cheek and
call us bitch and slut and whore and tease
and we will have you as we please
pleasure your ignorance with claws and teeth
and leave you blood-sworn in the streets
our pilgrimage to nature is not a joke
or cliché or dissipation in bonfire smoke

to bear the cities (in our throats)
to bear the grey (invade our hair)
to bear the men (who under pay)
we walk away to
wealth more green
to rope our homes among the trees
and sing our praises to open skies
and clear our grief free from disguise

Sisters!
let him speak
the man
the god
you

# BECKER

Should I be judged by the clothes that clothe my skin?
Eyes focused on what's out,
no thought of what's within.
A trackie means I'm on madness,
live below standards and know no manners.
Gonna come up in your face, curse, swear and scream.
Could've sworn on the good book that you saw the nine-inch gleam
'cause my fitted's on low,
you can't see my eyes,
gets you prang, can't eyewitness 'cause the face is disguised.
Boy or girl?
Imposs to tell.
Ambiguity throwing hot flushes, making you feel unwell,
stereotypes taking control,
hijacking your brain as we wait together for the District line train.
But 'cause I tap my feet to the hip-hop beat,
you assume I'm geared up and I'm packing heat.
Sound shoots your heart,
I'm on the other end,
the lyrics I spray you can't comprehend
'cause you jumped, stomach flipped as I said 'wagwan'.
Obvious that you can't relate to the platform that I'm on.
But it's not like you tried.
With the media's view of the streets you've complied.
Nothing natural 'bout how these niggas died.
Seem to've forgotten that it was your people
who originally supplied the weapons
that have now got you shook,
cautious they'll steal your essence with the craft of a crook.
Any sudden movement, panic makes you look,
ears sharply tuned to the silent sound of a jook.
Sensitive sense snaps back into reality.
Train's here, sausage-packed doors open in front of me,
so I
mind the gap,
find a gap, then deftly mould to fit.
As a brick in the wall I watch you as you mouth the word *shit*.
Sight sees the timer, it's an eight-minute wait,
there's no space for you now so you're gonna be late,
but I,
being me,
a contrast of what you perceive,
ask people to move in oh so politely.
A place is created, the space you invade.

Arrogance arises. Dominance displayed,
only for an announcement to erase your parade.
'I'm afraid to say, but your train is delayed.'
Demeanour demeaned. A nightmare it seems.
Disintegration of elegance, you're no longer pristine,
so you jump off the train a sec premature.
Ears failed to hear the signalling sound of the doors,
tucking me in safely.
I raise my head to see
you left behind, ignorant
of what becomes of my journey.

# FADE

It's funny how love fades away.
Imagine you could pinpoint every bruise
ever.
It's fortunate how love fades away.

# THIS TEXT: EQUALITY VS EQUITY

I suppose the text knows what it is made from
when it is asked    *what it is*.

It answers with what it contains.
This question taunts the text.

Ask the text questions it has the thoughts for.

Don't mock the text.
The text can't feel the
drone dumb reprints.

Leave the text flat.

Do not fail to cultivate the quality of the silence.

Don't title the text 'Lexicon'.
Text is not 'of or for words'.
They will carve their value worthless.

Watch them lick themselves clear of connotations.

Words witness too many things.
Their sentences hold weighted charges,
homophones
to
homographs,
even homonyms.

Ordinarily words
will mistake themselves for gospel.
Preach within    their form.
Believe their lines rule.
Words demand to be discovered discovering the new,
twist themselves upside down.
Stamped in different time zones.

Text is a symbol of the times
– more than its sum.

Algebraic riddles.
Calligraphic ellipsis.

To exist is as recent as a dictionary's birth.

Lines turned to letters,
seams of displaced alphabets
land, under breath.
The return to etymology – what I am?
Gentrified scrawls.
Ask the text what it thinks of equality.
It will reply,
*An equitable journey from source to hand,*
*all intention forcing through an undefined state of being,*
*a justified honesty in not knowing.*

# 1432

'I love you.'
Mind maximises effects of words I've heard escape from a mouth
borrowed and placed on my face,
'cause I've
felt this feeling before,
of more:
more time, touch, texts,
affectionate attention.
Too much is not enough.
But
it was lust.
Pure lust.

I'd lost sense and jumped into the endorphin mix
where courage and confidence were clumped together,
pumped with Cupid's drug and labelled love.
To me it was lovely.
But he was immune
and refused to consume from pit where boils would burst,
releasing statements that slipped out as easily as he
slipped in.
So,
'I love you'
brings me to when once silence answered back initially,
immediately
replaced by a 'me too' bear hug.
I thought bared words
worth more
than the cliché I'd sold for free.

'I love you.'
Drums pick up beat
of a heart
that's destined to be
torn apart
by a girl who's yet
to be hurled from past
into present.
A gift patiently waiting for the
stubborn child who threw tantrums at parents,
just in need of reassurance
that
Mother's insurance was for life,
not on loan

nor a replacement for a broken phone
or a Trocadero token
to be
traded in for the real win.

What am I thinking?
As legs sink into a hypochondriac's chair,
I'm scared.
So tough to 'I love you too.'
Let me flicker eyes with care, prepare the
'Me too'
echoed reply of what I received so long ago,
knowing it'll
resound as it rebounds in his mind.
I'm compulsively being kind
by cushioning with foam squares,
reused, resilient
right-angled truths,

as I return to my eight crumpled letters,
wondering whether
'I still' was really 'I never',
as our relationship was as rocky as the caramel chocolate bars our
skin colours matched.
And 'do' is really 'did',
'cause he did do the do,
digging deep inside a womb
to miscarry man's ignorance
which once grasped the sharp parts of a one-way mirror,
deceiving me to believe that the reflection of just one
was actually two.

Now I see only you.
Phantasmal to me,
and yet you pursue to fine-tune a
facsimile of my own broken record.

You say, 'I love you.'
I say $1 + 4 - 3 = 2$
(I love you too).

# POETRY AS PROTEST

*Click yourself on,*
*find your simmer.*
*Turn it high.*
*Now, write.*

Greenpeace just asked me
whether there are any other issues that concern me.
I can't say no.
So, retort,
'Rent and avocados and coffee.'

It's too deep for an online survey –
ask the click questions,
yes/no closed questions,
you write the choices and I agree. I mean,
is this a trick?
This 'help us help you' question,

believing that a remote opening of this mail-
out should be enough of a donation.

What do you want from me?
Of course there are.
Seriously!
What bigger symptom of powerlessness is there than
to huff at a charity that wants to save the world?
Haven't they earned my concern?

Don't you want to save our world?

Perhaps I should protest myself,
strike my face to wake my brain to this dark age,
march spears across skin numb to believing that this is humans
killing themselves,
that we live in the chaos of suicide,
that our rivers are arrested,
that our oceans are mourning,
that our trees are chain-smoking,

that none of those belong to us,

our possessive adjectives can't save us.

How is this a protest?

A placard poem.
A free write march.
An isolated share and crucified post.
Star of David in the infinity of Goliath.
I'm going off-piste.
They've asked for a blog on protest poetry, I've written a polemic.

What is a protest?
Is it an awareness campaign? Is it a banner of what we want
instead? Is it a rave? Is it a local store, a bed sheet slogan from
an estate marked for capital? Is it a palace in a shop doorway? A
squat, a ticket touter? A shoplifter? A fare jumper, fraud,
or is it silence? Is it turning your face for each slap? Is it gluttony,
leaving the tap to run? Accumulation and hoarding, refusing to
die, a flag, a soundbite, a vote. Surely protest has failed its terms.
Surely it's not an ideal candidate for this job of activation.
Accept the loss.

Hold your power.
There's a little bit of border in all of us,
manifested as decisions with enough shame to self-destruct.
Find the source of this truth,
the part of you which twitches at the barrage of syllables.

Click yourself on,
find your simmer.
Turn it high.
This gauge instinctively lowers itself in its own time,
the flow of thought will collide and console its selves in neural
paths.
Now, write.

Courageous visibility
of heart blood
to gather in chambers,
to give, to receive,
to come, to go,
to love and be love.

I delete the retort of 'poverty, water and energy sources'.
My greatest concern:
we don't believe that humans are capable of creating this.

# MATTER (EXCERPT)

*Before time and space, matter and energy were inseparable and everything that this universe has become was concentrated to a single incredibly tiny point, like an island in a never-ending ocean.*


The colour of light at the bottom of the ocean is red. No other
colour but red,
that's what Miss said Newton said,
the spectrum, he said, shows white light to be made up of every
other colour
shot through glass then split apart,
rainbows use rain as glass and sun as light
and we learnt that the Sun was a star,
*our star,*
and I knew about the solar eclipse
but I couldn't see it 'cause there were clouds, and the papers said
that there was a poisonous smog,
but I think they didn't want us to see it in real life 'cause it can turn
you blind
and some people say it's a portal like Narnia or the Northern Lights.
I've only seen the Northern Lights online.
@home the sky is purple and bruised like,
like our street lights are pummelling the inside of our atmosphere.


You only see the really bright stars or the moon or aeroplanes.
I make believe that they are shooting stars and wish on them.
My sister tells me to stop believing in wishes, she says they don't
come true.
I'm hoping she is wrong. I'm believing she is wrong.
Roald Dahl says that magic doesn't exist for people who don't
believe in it...
Well,    I believe in it.
I still say the traffic light spell to change the lights from red to green
and it works *all* of the time when I really concentrate and
believe in it


Illusions occur when our brains attempt to perceive the future
and these perceptions don't match reality.
Gregory showed me that even with knowledge and understanding
of what is 'real',
our brains will reject that in favour of what it thinks is correct to see.

'Nice fish.' Stop speaking. 'Fish, your fish is nice.'
Fish?! Stop, breathe.
Close eyes open, here by my side, eyes in mine, pacific blue,
rouge smile triangle of teeth – 'Great pet, your pet is great.'
Eyes roll back to white, mirrored crystals burning away any
coolness I never had.
I can't think quick, tsunami.
Centre stance to disappear.
Grin at this shark, defy the beat.
Sightline spans 360 degrees.
This is drowning, keep evolving.
Find your feet,
meteor lights crashing,
atoms smashing,
this is launching into battle,
this is bass-lining a black hole,
this is event horizon fading,
this is the time and space I've been sailing,
this is the surf my mouth is breaking.

It's *like*
it knows when my mind is not focused,
when I am just saying the words and I don't mean them and I have
to repeat them with feeling.

# ACKNOWLEDGEMENTS

Margaret Atwood. Björk. Mariah Carey.

All the people that inspired these words. Oh boys. Oh girls. Oh love.
All the stages. All the kindness.
All the roads. All the parks.
All the transport. All the booze.
Every smile, laugh and shiny eye.
Every moment of sad. Each punch of paper.

Browns Cru, Hot 2 Death, Sh!tS!ck, Rubix, Chill Pill, Point Blank Poets, Keats House... all the butterflies.

Christian McLaughlin for trusting me.

Lyric Hammersmith, Roundhouse Camden, NYT, Albany Deptford, New Writing South, Oval House, Young Vic.

Arts Council England, Kevin and Kate McGrath. Thank you for investing in me

Rosanna Hildyard for being the first editor to see and believe in this collection.

Special thanks to Becky Thomas for your determined patience with me.

Thank you, Burning Eye and Joanna Layla. Thanks so so so much

# NOTES ON THE POEMS

All were written between 2007 and 2017.

*How to Be a Feminist* was written in response to the trolling that Caroline Criado-Perez got on Twitter.

*Cog* was written in response to Lily Allen's 'Hard Out Here' video.

*iPhone* – massive thanks to the Chill Pill gents who sorted me out over summer 2012.

## Commissions:

*Read My Lips* written as part of a collaboration with Jacqui Beckford. Dir. Christian McLaughlin (2008)
*Nowadays A Road to Voting* (short film) (2010)
*Swift Key* Swift Key app (2014)
*Monopolised News* is 'People Like', BBC 1Xtra (2015)
*London Landlords The Guardian* (2015)
*Grow Wild* Kew Gardens (2016)
*Change, You Say On the Button* podcast
*Reconstruction* St Paul's Cathedral and Poet in the City (2016). Listen and say along! http://poetinthecity.co.uk/undertheskin/
*Poetry as Protest* British Council (2016)

## Reprints:

*Terminals* and *Silver Focus* first printed in *Podium Poets 1*: https://spread-the-word-london.myshopify.com/products/podium-poets

*Matter* a creative experiment into the relationship humans have with light. Funded by Arts Council England. To find out more check out www.thisismatter.com. 250 copies of the first draft available on Etsy: www.etsy.com/uk/shop/thisismatter

Thanks to you for getting to this point!